MW01126684

A Call to Friends: Faithful Living in Desperate Times

Marty Grundy

Inner Light Books
San Francisco, California
2020

A Call to Friends:
Faithful Living in Desperate Times

© 2020 Marty Grundy
All rights reserved

Editor: Charles Martin
Copy editor: Kathy McKay
Layout and design: Matt Kelsey

Published by Inner Light Books
San Francisco, California
www.innerlightbooks.com
editor@innerlightbooks.com

Library of Congress Control Number: 2020940425

ISBN 978–1–7346300–6–0 (hardcover)
ISBN 978–1–7346300–7–7 (paperback)
ISBN 978–1–7346300–8–4 (eBook)

Introduction

As I think of the ills of our times—the horrible things we humans inflict on ourselves, on each other, on pretty much all living things, and on the Earth itself—it seems to me that early Friends had the antidote we so desperately need. They experienced the simple—but extremely difficult—Truth that we are loved unconditionally and are called to live lives of integrity and love. Early Friends knew experientially that there was One who could guide them to live ever more faithfully into that which Jesus taught and demonstrated. Jesus called it the Kingdom of Heaven. Early Friends used a variety of terms but understood it required surrendering their self-will in order to discern and obey the Inward Guide teaching them how to create a more just and loving society. It occurs to me that perhaps too many Friends today have forgotten or lost sight of the radical call of these life-changing experiences. I want to try to describe for myself and others what Friends might again be able to experience ourselves and then offer to this hurting world.

This essay is an amalgam of two efforts. The first was the Bible Half Hours I offered at New England Yearly Meeting in August 2017 on that year's theme of Romans 12:2. The second was a workshop I co-facilitated with Connie Green at the Ben Lomond Quaker Center in California titled Faithful Living in Challenging Times. The "times"—in terms of the environmental catastrophe we humans are unleashing upon the Earth and all its creatures, the unravelling of what has passed for democracy in the United States and too many other nations, the systemic racism we live with, the official barbaric treatment by the United States of refugees and asylum seekers, the vicious wars and violence around the world often waged with weapons and other assistance from the United

States—are increasingly appalling. What are Friends to do?

When I was first approached with the possibility of leading the Bible Half Hours, my heart said "Yes!" I knew there was something I needed to say, especially about the terrible things we humans are doing to this beautiful, intricately interknit planet of which we are one part and that is our only home. As I meditated on the verse from Romans 12—*Do not be conformed to this world, but be transformed by the renewal of your minds, so that you may discern what is the will of God— what is good and acceptable and perfect* (NRSV)—my prayer became, "What does thee want to say to New England Friends through me?" I continued to live with this verse in a variety of translations.

Connie Green and I have been yokefellows with complementary gifts since the 1990s, working together in ongoing spiritual discussion groups in Cleveland Meeting and traveling together among Friends. So, when I was approached by Ben Lomond to offer a retreat there, I immediately asked if Connie could facilitate it with me. Unfortunately, since we have moved to opposite coasts we have gotten out of practice working together with the Spirit. We inexplicably jettisoned our carefully prepared notes, and the program at Ben Lomond was not what it should have been for the participants. This essay comes as an effort to put into writing what I hoped—but failed—to convey there.

Because the Bible and early Friends are among my sources, I tend to reflect their language by using words such as "God," "Christ," "Kingdom of Heaven," and so on. By God I do not mean an old man with a white beard sitting on a cloud. I am talking about that Something that is both immanent and transcendent, within us and beyond us. I am talking about the Creative Energy holding the universe together, the Cosmic Love that is a bedrock experience or yearning for most humans through time and across cultures. Other terms might be Spirit, Higher Power, Eternal Now, Ground of Our Being, and Inward Light. When I use Christ, I am not trying to give a surname to Jesus of Nazareth. Other translations are Logos, Light, Seed, and Creative Energy. Yes, there is a lack of fine theological differentiation as the understandings of God and Christ overlap. I am not a Trinitarian, and the term and concept of the Trinity do not appear in the Bible or as part of the experience of early Friends. My sense is that when individuals in the early Jesus movement experienced the Presence in a variety of ways, they groped for metaphors to describe it: like a father, or through Jesus, or in the presence of community. When the actual experiences grew dim, the felt need to hold fast to correct wordings led to dogmatic assertions, and differing from these became heresy. Please develop and use your own translations for these terms, remembering this simple ditty:

> Whatever idea your mind comes at
> I tell you flat
> God is *not* that.[1]

About the Author

Born into a Quaker family with roots going back to the 1650s, as a teenager Marty Grundy loved reading about early Friends. The thing that puzzled her was that they seemed so alive and on fire; they willingly risked and endured small and large deprivations and sufferings for Something so much bigger than themselves that was obviously filling them with joy and courage. Even though a few men in her meeting had served in Civilian Public Service camps during World War II, nobody she knew seemed to be suffering or doing anything extraordinary.[2] She was not at all sure that her meetings for worship were so electric that they would have sustained her through having things unjustly seized, being beaten, or her parents being put in jail. What was the difference between early Friends and Friends today?

Thus began a long and meandering journey to learn more about her spiritual ancestors. This involved learning to read seventeenth-century handwriting in order to decipher old meeting minutes. She became able to translate old grammar and syntax. Then it became necessary to learn their language of metaphor, which was based on the Bible. So, she read and studied the Bible. She read the writings of more recent Friends as well as earlier ones. In graduate school she wrote on the choices made by individual Friends in family groups over four generations in one rural Pennsylvania meeting between 1750 and 1850. Over the years Marty has come to feel that she's been given a vision of what the Religious Society of Friends has been and could be again.

In the 1980s she became involved with the Religious Education Committee of Friends General Conference (FGC), with a particular interest in adult religious education. She served the committee as recording clerk for many years, as well as recording for FGC's Central

About the Author

Committee. Marty began being asked to travel among Friends to lead workshops and retreats, and occasionally offered talks at yearly meeting sessions. This culminated in 1998 when she was asked to serve as the first clerk of the Traveling Ministries Program of FGC.

Marty has also written for both scholarly and religious publications. In particular, she has written a number of articles and more than sixty book reviews for *Friends Journal*.

She grew up in Southampton Meeting, Philadelphia Yearly Meeting; spent many years as a member of Cleveland Meeting, Lake Erie Yearly Meeting, which until 1993 was jointly affiliated with Ohio Yearly Meeting (Conservative); and now is a member of Wellesley Meeting, New England Yearly Meeting. She is married to Ken Grundy, and they have three grown children and a pair of grandtwins.

A Call to Friends: Faithful Living in Desperate Times

A Look at Our "Desperate Times"

Desperate times have recurred throughout history, most often symbolized by the four horsemen of the apocalypse: pestilence, war, famine, and death.[3] All of these are happening in the world right now, but we who are middle- and upper-middle-class white North Americans have been seemingly immune from them. Suddenly, the novel coronavirus has dismantled our assumed protection and exceptionalism. As citizens of a self-designated democracy, we in the United States continue to have some responsibility for the fact that the Empire—the United States Empire—is responsible for too much of the suffering around the world. The systems we tacitly accept here at home are increasingly exposed as unjust, racist, and immoral.

What makes our time different from previous times of desperation is the human destruction of the environment. From our theology of "subduing" the Earth[4] to our economic, political, and social systems of amassing financial profit and the political and social power that accompany great wealth with too little regard for the impact of our acquisitiveness (market capitalism), humans have unleashed global warming and the sixth great extinction. We have passed the tipping point, feedback loops are in full play, and the ecosystems that enable much of human and other life to thrive are being destroyed.

1

How can we respond? *Do not conform to the pattern of this world* (Romans 12:2 NIV), Paul implores us in his letter to the Romans. Let's take a look at this world we are urged not to conform to, not to be co-opted or seduced by, not to accommodate to. The first step in confronting violence or racism or exploitation is awareness—remaining attentive to life even in the midst of banality, heedlessness, and brutality.[5]

In this translation Paul specifically warns us about the *pattern* of this world. It isn't just a series of negative incidents; there is a pattern to them, and this pattern is what we are to recognize and reject. "Pattern" is another name for "system." Systems are made by humans, not by Divine design or fiat.[6]

I hardly know where to begin to name the patterns, systems, and cultural structures that enmesh us. As a Quaker historian, I'll point to a few that may be buzzwords for some or unfamiliar concepts to others: the Doctrine of Discovery; colonialist mentality; subduing the Earth; social Darwinism; Ayn Rand's objectivism; inequality and injustice; the sixth great extinction; hubris and anthropocentrism in our attitude toward the Earth and all living things; racism and white supremacy distorting the legal, prison, education, employment, housing, and health systems; homophobia and attacks on transgender and other people perceived as "different" and therefore to be feared and loathed; sexism, classism, able-ism, xenophobia, and all the ways humans categorize and diminish one another; commodification of everything that can possibly be reduced to a dollar value to enable some individual or entity to make a profit; obvious and blatant corruption in high places setting the tone that only fools obey the law, that helping one another is for suckers; conscious deliberate destruction of "the commons" that should be held for the good of the entire populace as well as for other creatures, most obviously in terms of the air, water, soil, pure food, and safe, effective medicines we need to survive, in addition to our national parks, forests, monuments and protected natural areas; twisting the care of ill fellow humans into a profit-driven enterprise as well as scalping protective gear and medicine in times of pandemic; bellicose statements inflaming tension with North Korea, Iran, Russia, and even Cuba; and yet another young black man murdered by police, another immigrant family torn apart, another desperate refugee family denied asylum while fleeing violence stoked by US policies and arms sales. The United States, in too many ways, is leading the world on this destructive, selfish, short-sighted, violent, racist path.

It is critical that we examine our times and cry out about what is happening all around us—piercing through the numbness, joining with those who are caught in the depths of it, and grieving. Grief is the antidote to the numbness that is the condition that the Empire prefers us to be in.[7] Albert Schweitzer, a major hero of my childhood, is reported to have pleaded, "Think occasionally of the suffering of which you spare yourself the sight." In Lloyd Lee Wilson's memorable phrase, we are members of the "implicated resistance," and it should keep us humble to remember how much we profit from the system we resist.[8]

Lamentation

If you feel your eyes stinging, if you want to pour out a lamentation, go ahead. Tears can cut through where reason and arguments beg to be refuted or "managed" by going numb. Tears wash away the numbness. Tears are a necessary first step. There can be no healing without grieving. "Such grief denies denial its power to look away in desperate pursuit of healing."[9]

As a Friend, in some ways I am no longer at home in

3

this nation whose administration seems intent on destroying the protections (weak as some of them were) for just about everything I hold dear. The liberation theologian Robert McAfee Brown used Psalm 137 to describe the sense of desolation and despair of the exiled Israelites and of people today, and I take the following exegesis of the psalm from him.[10]

When the Jews were exiled, some settled in Babylon, and they wailed, "How shall we sing the Lord's song in a foreign land?" Sometimes our memories of what has been and what could be, compared to the awfulness of the present, overwhelm us, and all we seem able to do is weep.

By the rivers of Babylon—there we sat down and there we wept when we remembered Zion. (NRSV)

At least weeping is an honest facing of how we feel. Sometimes it alternates with silence, which may be a refusal to face the destruction and sorrow around us.

On the willows there we hung up our harps.

We cannot sing at all. Around us, others may demand that we pretend to be happy, to stop being so negative, to get a grip. They ask us to buy the fallacy of the privileged that claims that since we, the privileged, have not been personally hurt, it is irrelevant that all around us other people are hurting and the earth is being destroyed.

For there our captors asked us for songs, and our tormentors asked for mirth, saying, "Sing us one of the songs of Zion!"

When this pretense only makes matters worse, we are faced with devastation. We poignantly ask, *"How could we sing the Lord's song in a foreign land?"* and the answer is, We can't.

But devastation is not the final word. Amazingly, the

psalmist changes the mood. Now, our memories are to galvanize us. We are to write them down so they will endure and others will be empowered by them. Our right hand (the writing hand) deserves to wither if we forget, and our voices will be struck mute if we do not speak of that which those who hold us captive scorn. Let us today remember the example of early Friends, even as those Friends remembered Jesus and the psalmist remembered Jerusalem.

> *If I forget you, O Jerusalem, let my right hand wither! Let my tongue cling to the roof of my mouth, if I do not remember you, if I do not set Jerusalem above my highest joy.*

The psalmist is rallying, calling not only on the people to remember but also calling to God to remember. As Paul said later (Romans 8:31 KJV), *If God be for us, who can be against us?*

> *Remember, O Lord, against the Edomites the day of Jerusalem's fall, and how they said "Tear it down! Tear it down! Down to its foundations!"*

We must remember—meaning that we must, in John Heagle's words, be "willing to live with conscious intentionality and to carry the consequences of our history."[11] We must grieve, but we must do more. It is an act of courage to remember our collective history in a world of cultural amnesia. Remember the things done in our name as citizens of the Empire or as members of the Religious Society of Friends. Grieve, and do not forget.

And then the whole thing comes unraveled in the psalm. For what end are the memories to be preserved? For revenge. We'll get even, even bashing out the brains of the Babylonians' children on the nearest rock.

This is reprehensible. But have we ever felt so angry? So furious at the unfairness of it all? We are angry about the innocents who are being killed so carelessly and wantonly; police walking away from yet another murdered black youth; the deliberate greedy slaughter of intelligent social animals such as whales or elephants with their intricate, caring relationships a few ("Western") humans are finally beginning to recognize;[12] the desperate refugees turned away; the murdered people written off as "collateral damage"; mountaintops blown off and toxic rubble dumped into mountain streams; officials appointed to pervert and dismantle agencies intended to serve the wider good; leadership that does not lead for the common good; a system of debt that traps and keeps individuals in poverty; the headlong rush to extract all the fossil fuels possible and build all the pipelines and infrastructure before a shift in political winds reduces their profit potential; a jury once again accepting the argument that a murder is justified if the police officer merely *thought* he was in danger. Let's clench our fists and teeth and acknowledge the rush of adrenaline. Aaaargh!

Once we have admitted the universal humanness of these feelings—including our own anger—the strong passions must be transmuted into moral outrage that is carefully channeled into positive, nonviolent action for change or it will degenerate into soul-destroying bloodthirsty revenge.[13] Put another way, we must lay aside the revenge of unredeemed anger of Psalm 137 in light of the larger message of the Bible. We turn, instead, to Isaiah 61:1–4 (NIV):

> *The Spirit of the Sovereign LORD is on me,*
> *because the LORD has anointed me*
> *to proclaim good news to the poor.*
> *He has sent me to bind up the brokenhearted,*
> *to proclaim freedom for the captives*
> *and release from darkness for the prisoners,*
> *to proclaim the year of the LORD's favor*
> *and the day of vengeance of our God,*

to comfort all who mourn,
  and provide for those who grieve in Zion—
to bestow on them a crown of beauty
  instead of ashes,
the oil of joy
  instead of mourning,
and a garment of praise
  instead of a spirit of despair.
They will be called oaks of righteousness,
  a planting of the LORD
  for the display of his splendor.
They will rebuild the ancient ruins
  and restore the places long devastated;
they will renew the ruined cities
  that have been devastated for generations.

The setting in Isaiah is the same as in Psalm 137: the Hebrews are once again in exile. Things look hopeless. But this time the end is not revenge. It is a manifesto of hope. What's the difference? The author's faith is not based in vengeance but in the greatness of God. This is the God of justice who brought the enslaved people out of Egypt. Since God is just, there is hope that God will intervene again and see to it that in God's universe, justice eventually prevails. The first verse and a half are familiar because they are the words Jesus used to begin his ministry. The first half of the second verse, "to proclaim the year of the Lord's favor," seems to have been echoed by George Fox, who felt called "to sound the day of the Lord" at the top of Pendle Hill in 1652.[14]

What is the cause of the change between Psalm 137 and Isaiah 61? The change comes through embracing the faith that reversal is possible, that justice will prevail over injustice. Why? Because the Spirit of the Lord is upon us, because God has appointed us to preach good tidings to the afflicted. God is at work here. Second, if this is what God wills, then we are to roll up our sleeves and help make it happen. God wants justice? Then we must act justly. God wants the ancient ruins rebuilt? Then let's get out a hammer and saw and get to work. God wants to comfort those who mourn? Then we ourselves must comfort others. We are to share with others a new vision, a new hope. We must imagine a new vision—and act upon it.

A grief exercise

But what about our grief? This country, in particular, seems heavy with grief, grief that is neither faced nor named. Consequently, it manifests in depression, suicide, addiction, projection, and violence. Francis Weller, a psychotherapist, writer, and soul activist, has done a lot of work helping people heal their grief. In the words of Kathleen Dean Moore, "Even though sorrow never disappears, it can make a deeper connection to the currents of life and so connect, somehow, to sources of wonder and solace."[15]

Weller names five "gates" into deep grief. One of them is what is happening to the world, to the ecosystems of the Earth and within the sociopolitical system in which we live.

> Whether or not we consciously recognize it, the daily diminishment of species, habitats, and cultures is noted in our psyches. Much of the grief we carry is not personal, but shared, communal. It is difficult to walk down the street and not feel the collective sorrows of homelessness or the economic insanity revealed in commercialism and consumerism.[16]

Although early Friends deliberately eschewed rituals that had become mechanical charades, Weller believes that from our earliest evolution humans are wired to participate in rituals at the critical points in life. Therefore, he has developed retreats that incorporate grief rituals.[17] Borrowing a simplified version, during a retreat at Ben Lomond Quaker Center in February 2019, Connie Green and I experimented with facilitating an exercise. A large bowl of water surrounded with some natural greenery was placed in the center of the circle. Near it were placed several dozen small, rough stones. Each participant was invited to pick up one or more stones, name the sorrow it represented, and place it in the bowl of water. We named the death of a loved one, the old shame of never-forgotten acts, the clear-cutting and burning of the Amazonian rain forest, hopes that went unfulfilled, the destruction of indigenous ways of relating to nature, old family dysfunctions, and the precipitous collapse of insect populations, coral reefs, and so many glaciers. We tasted the grief. Then a young man carefully carried the bowl outdoors and poured the water at the base of a tree so that our grief might be transmuted into something useful. A woman offered to take the stones and carry them to the edge of the ocean. There, she carefully placed them, naming all the persons who had participated, allowing the natural action of the waves and water to gradually wear off the roughness and make each stone smooth.

There are other ways of dealing with grief, both as individuals and, more importantly, as a group. It seems critical for our mental and spiritual and social health to acknowledge our grief, express it, and find some way that we can learn to live on the far side of it.

A Different Paradigm

What are Friends to do in this situation, these times in which we live? If we are able to constructively deal with anger and grief, what else is required? I am pleased to say that many Friends are already very involved in a wide variety of social justice and environmental work. Friends are engaged in prison ministry; feeding and working with the "underhoused"; struggling to understand and diminish white privilege and racism; opposing pipelines and the institutions that finance extraction of yet more fossil fuels, including mountaintop removal; working with immigrants and refugees; supporting LGBTQ+ folks; encouraging the use of solar and wind power and considering the ways we could use less fossil fuel; supporting efforts to reverse the undoing of nuclear proliferation and anti-ballistic missile treaties; working for a decent minimum wage; caring for wild places; supporting the efforts of the Friends Committee on National Legislation to influence Congress and the administration to advance peace, justice, equal opportunities, and environmental stewardship—and so much more that I have not mentioned.

But more is required of us. What is required is not more hours working at the soup kitchen or with Alternatives to Violence workshops or picketing corporate headquarters or any of the myriad other ways Friends are deeply involved in peace, social justice, and environmental work. These are good and important ways to serve, and they need to continue. In addition to these—not in place of them—what is required is a shift in our way of doing these important activities, a paradigm shift in the way we think about the world. As a religious society, we need a deepening relation with the Holy Spirit. We need a vision of a different way to organize society that is not inherently exploitative and hierarchical. New economic and political systems can evolve from a Spirit-inspired vision of a different social system.

What is this deeper relation with the Spirit that inspires a new vision? To be able to articulate it, I go back to early Friends and what they realized was being asked of them. They preached that Christ is come to teach his people himself.[18] And what is Christ, the Logos, the In-ward Light, Creative Energy[19] teaching this gathered people—us? To more clearly understand that, we need to go back to look at what Jesus of Nazareth was teaching the people of his time in Palestine under the crushing power of the Roman Empire. Then, we'll look at some ways we might prepare ourselves to be more open to a deeper relation with God's Spirit and how this might be reflected in our meetings as they become genuine, strong faith communities.

The kingdom Jesus taught

In some interesting ways, Jesus lived under condi-tions that mirror ours. In other ways, of course, our times are quite different. Empires—the Roman and the United States—use political, military, and economic power to coerce subject peoples to give the Empire the resources it covets. Society is constructed in ways that support the Empire and seem to be immutable. Life for middle and upper classes in the metropole could/can be quite civilized and pleasant; life for nearly everyone else was/is grim.

Jesus spoke a great deal about what he called the "Kingdom of Heaven" or the "Kingdom of God." He probably purposely chose a word rich with political meaning in order to juxtapose the experienced reality of inequality and injustice in the political "kingdom" of the Herodean monarchs and the Roman Caesars with the vision he held up of a radically different system under the leadership of God.[20]

Let's go back to the time of Jesus and look at the way humans organized relationships among people back then. This was a society that people assumed was inher-ent and unchangeable. In contrast, we'll also look at what Jesus was proposing—and actually demonstrating.

A Call to Friends

Two millennia ago, there were two main constructs controlling the way people saw themselves and interacted with others. These two ideas were not unique to the eastern Mediterranean. They informed practically all human societies that were more formally organized than the freedom and equality which hunter-gatherers enjoyed.[21] These ideas still control life in much of the world today. These two powerful ideas can be identified with the paired terms "honor/shame" and "patron/client."

It took me a while to get my head around the idea that "honor" in this context does not mean integrity or trustworthiness or self-respect. In this context, it means the reputation and respect one person can demand from another. It's all about face. Its corollary is shame—when a person cannot command respect and is disrespected, reviled, and no longer accepted as a welcome part of the "in group." Honor has to do with power, power over others. It is competitive, zero-sum, and breeds violence.[22]

The other major construct, intimately connected with the first, is the system of patronage and clientage. A strong person or family collects clients—people and families that give him (rarely her) or them respect in return for protection and occasional favors. Strong clients collect weaker clients and on down the social hierarchy. A broker can mediate between patrons and clients, creating a comfortable and remunerative niche. You might recognize this as the feudal system across medieval Europe, but it still exists. This system, too, is about power; the patron has power over clients, larger clients have power over weaker clients, and so on down the line. It is also competitive, zero-sum, and breeds violence. Not unexpectedly, economics is an important part of the system, breeding gross inequality.

At the time of Jesus, these twin systems were firmly entrenched. People could easily assume that they were inevitable and immutable—that's just the way life was, and it could not be any other way. The games of honor were played by a very small percentage of the wealthy population, especially the Roman imperialists and their clients among the elites of the subject populations. The patronage game trickled down all the way to the peasants, who were lowly clients of a landlord, a money lender, or simply someone who was more powerful. In this system, someone who was destitute was cast out of the system without resources, without worth, and most certainly without honor.

Into this mess strode Jesus of Nazareth, son of a carpenter. Carpenters, by the way, were not the valued tradesmen we might assume such skilled artisans to be; they had no land, and they were lumped in with lowly peasants. John Dominic Crossan has described the twin roots of Jesus' teaching. Jesus didn't only preach a new way—he lived it, and his followers demonstrated it in their daily lives. One part of his revolutionary ministry was free healing done in people's homes and villages but not in specific places that could develop a system of patrons, brokers, and clients. Think of the economics of medieval pilgrimage sites, let alone the medical industry conglomerates in the United States today. The other part of Jesus' revolutionary ministry was his practice of an open table that welcomed everyone and anyone to eat together, disregarding honor, custom, and status. This combination of healing and eating, as Crossan explains,

> was a challenge launched not just on the level of Judaism's strictest purity regulations, or even on that of the Mediterranean's patriarchal combination of honor and shame, patronage and clientage, but at the most basic level of civilization's eternal inclination to draw lines, invoke boundaries, establish hierarchies, and maintain discriminations. It did not invite a political revolution but envisaged a social one at the imagination's most dangerous depths.[23]

The Brazilian Presbyterian liberation theologian Rubem Alves urges us to grasp "the insight that Imagination is more real, and Reality less real, than it looks."[24] Any fundamental change in the social order must begin with imagining something different.

It isn't recorded that Jesus talked about transformation per se. But what else could enable people to actually live into his invitation to God's Kingdom? How can someone discard the ingrained mental constructs of shame and clientage and become emotionally, psychologically, and spiritually strong and free enough to accept and to be accepted as an equal to every other person—male and female, pagan and observant Jew, learned scholar and illiterate peasant, violent revolutionary and political collaborator, and all the other differences we delight in reinforcing? How can one be open to this stunning change without being transformed—regardless of the terminology?

It is good to remember, as Gayle Erwin notes, that "no theology is of any threat or consequence until we try to apply it to our lives."[25]

Mennonite John Howard Yoder picks up on another strand of what Jesus was offering to the people—and what made him such a threat to the authorities. Yoder uses the gospel of Luke to make his point, at least in part because Luke was trying to convince the Romans that the young Christian movement was quite harmless, a mere "spiritual" group. So, it is interesting to follow Yoder as he teases out of Luke's account the earlier strands of tradition that tell quite a different story.[26]

When Jesus began his ministry, his gospel, he proclaimed:

The Spirit of the Lord is upon me, because he hath anointed me to preach the gospel to the poor; he hath sent me to heal the brokenhearted, to preach deliver-

ance to the captives, and recovering of sight to the blind, to set at liberty them that are bruised, to preach the acceptable year of the Lord. (Luke 4:18–19 KJV)

This "acceptable year of the Lord" would have been understood by his hearers as Jubilee. Scholars debate whether the every-fiftieth-year Jubilee ever happened in its fullness, but apparently enough happened that people were familiar with it and that elite minds had developed clever work-arounds for those who already had more than their share and intended to hold on to it—namely, those who had loaned money that Jubilee would make uncollectable. Leviticus 25:8–17 and Isaiah 61 held out the prophetic hope of Jubilee, the promise of a time when debts would be erased, economic inequalities eliminated, and all God's people would start over again at the same point. It was tried at least once, at least the part about freeing slaves, when King Zedekiah proclaimed liberty to all Hebrew slaves. One way or another, however, the wealthy Hebrew enslavers took them back, causing Jeremiah to warn them that because of their failure to live up to the covenant with the God who had brought them out of slavery in Egypt, Jerusalem would fall to Nebuchadnezzar (34:8–17)—which it did.[27]

Of the four major parts of Jubilee, one was liberty for those enslaved and another was remission of debts. This was a major concern of Jesus, and the Lord's Prayer meant literally "remit us our debts as we ourselves have remitted them to our debtors." In other words, Jesus was saying to practice Jubilee; those who practiced grace would receive grace.

The parable of the merciless servant told a story well known by Jesus' peasant audience. Herod had instituted heavy taxation so that a peasant would have to borrow money to pay it, mortgaging his land. The interest on the debt climbed, the land was seized, and the trapped peasant became a sharecropper on his former land and then a servant. The interest kept mounting, and eventually he, his wife, and their children would be sold into slavery to cover the debt. With Jubilee in the form of the king in the parable forgiving his debt, the ungrateful servant then turned around and refused to grant Jubilee to his fellow slave. The moral of the story is that there will be no divine Jubilee for those who refuse to practice it on Earth.[28] This is probably meant descriptively rather than prescriptively. One can ponder the result of debt in the United States—intended or unintended—for student loans carefully excluded from bankruptcy protection and payday lenders with their exorbitant interest rates who are excluded from consumer protection regulations.

There is more. For instance, the parable of the dishonest steward is puzzling when removed from the context of the inequalities of peasant life in Palestine. Here, the dishonest steward was caught; his master demanded a reckoning. He knew he could never reimburse all he had embezzled. Instead, realizing that he would be put out of his comfortable job but was too weak for manual labor and too ashamed to beg, he thought of a way to ingratiate himself with the community which up to then had had good reason to loathe him. He called in each of the debtors and reduced their debts. When his master (perhaps standing in for God) learned of it, he commended the steward. The point of the parable seems to be that being an accepted part of the peasant community was of much greater value than ill-gotten wealth.[29] We'll look more at the role of community later.

Jubilee did not just mean the rich should give back. It also meant the poor should pay their just debts honestly—not waiting for Jubilee to give them a free ride. According to Leviticus, *You shall not cheat one another* (25:17a NRSV). In the light of these parables, what was the economic plan of Jesus? It seemed to be about Jubilee, not about setting up a commune nor giving a set of rules for an Essene-like community. Jubilee required both those who loaned and those who borrowed to honestly follow the most truthful and loving path.[30]

In one story, Luke 12:58–59, Jesus is recorded as saying that if you are being taken to court, *on the way make an effort to settle the case, or you may be dragged before the judge, and the judge [will] hand you over to the officer, and the officer throw you in prison. I tell you, you will never get out until you have paid the very last penny* (NRSV). The peasants who heard Jesus knew from bitter experience that this was true.

Another story says that if you are sued and your coat is demanded, give also your cloak (Matthew 5:40). This is enlarged for us by Walter Wink's understanding of what Jesus was saying here about debt. If you give both your coat and your cloak, Wink explains, you will be naked, and the Jew who looks at a naked man is shamed—not the one who is demonstrating the harsh injustice of the system. In addition, ancient Jewish law had decreed that if you took a man's cloak for debt, you had to give it back to him at night to enable him to keep himself warm.

Faced with the domination system that made up the Roman Empire with all its injustices and inequalities known up close and personal by the peasants of Palestine, what did Jesus feel was God's will for him to preach and demonstrate? First, what was he not asked to do? He was not asked to come up with an alternative political and economic system. Instead, he was asked to preach and model a new *social* system based on transformed hearts and renewed minds. He was to create a social revolution based on equality, honesty, and fair dealing in which all would have enough and none would have excess. Try to imagine how the world's political and economic systems might have changed if the social revolution that Jesus started had been allowed to blossom into its fullness. All too soon, theological doctrine and power-wielding institutional hierarchies undermined his testimony. But the original witness was unleashed and, although continually subverted, continues to beckon.

As English Quaker Mabel Dearmer (1872–1915) wrote,

> To the Greeks foolishness, to the Jews a stumbling-block [1 Corinthians 1:23]. Christianity can never teach common sense. It teaches the Kingdom of Heaven. It may permeate common sense with a tincture of its ideals, but the more common-sensible it becomes, the less is it Christianity. It is the folly only possible to the supremely wise.[31]

The radically egalitarian way of living together that Jesus introduced, suffused with hope, joy, and love, was powerfully attractive. People hungered for this close, loving, spiritual, and human relationship; in spite of persecution, people flocked to it. Tertullian wrote that the Romans were amazed and said "see how they love one another."

But, as we know, it didn't last. All too soon, even while the epistles and gospels were being written, individual leaders and factions were jockeying for power within and among early proto-Christian communities. With the actions and doctrines of Constantine and Augustine, the game was over, and all too soon the Jesus movement had become an institution that took on the characteristics of the Empire Jesus was resisting. This isn't the time or place to go into the "long dark night of apostasy," as George Fox bluntly named the institutionalized religion that developed between the time of the apostles and the inbreaking of the Friends' message. Nor is this the time to mention the tireless efforts of the Holy Spirit to bring God's Truth to each generation anew.

The insights and experience of early Friends

As mentioned above, George Fox summarized his openings as "Christ is come to teach his people himself," and what Christ was—and is—teaching is about living in that same "kingdom" in which Jesus preached and lived. In the seventeenth century, people understood the concept of "kingdom"—even, or especially, as they engaged in a civil war against the monarchy and decapitated the king. What is the salient issue in a kingdom? One is under the power and rule of a king.[32] Twenty-first-century Friends live in what purports to be a democracy and don't much like the concept of obedience to an outward authority. How, then, can we talk about this concept, which is critical to the understanding of both Jesus and early Friends? We'll come back to this later; for now, let's take a look at what early Friends were teaching and living.

From Fox's critical opening that "there is one even Christ Jesus who can speak to thy condition"[33] to his vision on Pendle Hill of "a great people to be gathered,"[34] it became clear to him—and to those who heard his prophetic message—that they were being invited to participate in a revival of "primitive Christianity." Empowered by the Spirit of the Living Christ within each of them and among the gathered group, they were to begin living in that Kingdom of which Jesus taught. This is precisely what Fox meant in his epistle to Friends:

> This is the word of the Lord God to you all and a charge to you all in the presence of the living God: be patterns, be examples . . . wherever you come; that your carriage and life may preach among all sorts of people, and to them.[35]

We are reminded by Norman J. Whitney that

the way to follow prophets is not to repeat what they said in past ages but to recapture what they meant in relation to the present.

New Conditions call, not for new principles but for a fresh vocabulary; Truth is still truth but each generation has the responsibility of restating the eternal in terms of the contemporary.

No one can be possessed of a profound Truth without seeking to communicate it; no one can be possessed by an overwhelming Love without the need to share it.[36]

Just as what Jesus taught was in marked opposition to the social, economic, and political systems of his day, so early Friends realized that the Spirit was asking them to live in marked opposition to the social, economic, and political systems of their day. We have no idea whether early followers of Jesus gave their cloaks as well as their coats in debtors' court, but we do know that they ate together, in flagrant opposition to religious and social regulations.

We are familiar with the symbolically powerful actions that early Friends took. God's Kingdom was not a hierarchy or a patriarchy, so those living in it did not take off their hats or bow or address with the plural "you" those whom the system deemed were superior and deserving of respect. They also eschewed the gold buttons, lace collars, and other sartorial representations of wealth and status. Jesus commanded, *Do not swear at all. . . . Let your word be 'Yes, Yes' or 'No, No'* (Matthew 5:33–37 NRSV), so that is what Friends did. They refused the double standard of an oath in court that implied this time they really would tell the truth. They boldly met together to worship, even when such gatherings were made illegal. They pioneered fair pricing for goods sold in their shops, refusing to bargain.[37]

These outward witnesses to the power and centrality of God's Kingdom in the lives of early Friends are what we mostly remember now, splitting each one into a separate "testimony." We forget that early Friends had a single testimony: their entire life, 24/7, demonstrating, modeling what living together in that Kingdom was like. It was a corporate enterprise. A person was acknowledged and recognized as a Friend when he or she upheld Friends' witness to that new social system. It wasn't about using the correct theological phrases, and it wasn't about selecting one or two "testimonies" with which one felt most comfortable. It was about living—in one's "measure," as one was able—into a new paradigm.

The prophetic stance/voice/witness of early Friends proclaimed that the Inward Light of Christ—available to all—led them to lives that preached. Their quotidian behavior, even more than their words, reached to the witness of God in others, demonstrating life in the Kingdom that Jesus taught.

At the First World Conference of Friends held in 1920, Friends declared that

> "Christianity involves living, even at this imperfect stage, as though the kingdom of God had come, and as though Love were the supreme force of life." They realised the necessity of having "a nucleus of people who practice it here, in this very difficult world, who have faith enough in it to make a venture and experiment of trying it, of living by it and, if need be, dying for it."[38]

As the 1952 Third World Conference concluded, "What we need to-day is not a new message, but new lives."[39]

Friends are not the only ones who see that the current systems are corrupt and unsustainable. Environmental journalists Dahr Jamail and Barbara Cecil have written,

Perhaps one of the most potent rebellions of this time is the refusal to walk in the mainstream western herd, conforming to expectations and values that have ultimately ravaged the Earth. Opting out at its core means realignment with an inner knowing about what is ours to do, from the inside out.[40]

Friends are familiar with what this "inner knowing" means, and one of our core tenets is to pay careful attention to it and increasingly follow its guidance. Friends have written extensively on discernment and on recognizing and following leadings. We hold workshops and retreats on these topics. We encourage one another in both these spiritual practices.

Spiritual practices

It seems unlikely that we will be able to sail smoothly through the uncharted and stormy seas ahead of us if we have no experience with boats. We need to learn how to navigate and how to trim the sails. When the wind and rain lash upon us on the open deck, it doesn't work to search for a how-to book and begin reading. We need to have had a lot of practice, apprenticeships, and experience. To shift metaphors, the more challenging the times become, the more we need strong spiritual "muscles" in order to do the work required of us. This demands the discipline of learning and practicing. One way to strengthen those muscles is through regular spiritual practices. Patricia Loring's helpful *Listening Spirituality, Vol. I: Personal Spiritual Practices among Friends* is an excellent place to begin if you are not already engaged in spiritual muscle-building. Another resource is Richard Foster's book *Spiritual Disciplines*.

There is no one-size-fits-all spiritual practice for Friends. As noted by Loring and Foster, there is a plethora of methods or disciplines that can be practiced. Probably the single most important factor is one's intention. Am I doing this to open myself—to leave my soul ajar, as Emily Dickinson wrote—to the love and presence and guidance of That Which Is Within and Beyond Me? If that is what I yearn for, if it is my heartfelt intention, and I follow a practice diligently, it may not matter so much which particular discipline I choose. What is called for is "hard work, self-sacrifice, a sense of balance, the humility to learn from our mistakes, courage and the heroic quality of meekness."[41]

Quoting from Thomas Kelly, a Quaker writing in the first half of the twentieth century,

> What is urged here are inward practices of the mind at deepest levels, letting it swing like the needle, to the polestar of the soul. And like the needle, the Inward Light becomes the truest guide of life, showing us new and unsuspected defects in ourselves and our fellows, showing us new and unsuspected possibilities in the power and life of good will among [humans].[42]

Allowing ourselves to be guided by the Inward Light does not happen easily or automatically—for us or for our spiritual ancestors. It helps to remember that in the midst of the political and social upheaval, religious questioning, and civil war of the mid-seventeenth century, plus the plague of 1665, most people who became Friends were already consciously hungry, seeking a deeper spiritual understanding and life. They described it as being worked on internally by the Holy Spirit/God, or they used some other metaphor. Then at a public meeting they heard a Quaker preach, and the words reached and connected with the witness or Seed or "that of God" already at work within them. This was often followed up with a session of private, intense, small group or one-on-one ministry. There might be no more contact with Friends until perhaps a different Friend would come through the area and clinch the convincement. Sometimes there was correspondence. However, it was always clear that new Friends, as well as more experienced ones, were to be taken to the feet of Christ and left there to learn from the Inward Teacher itself. What made those early Friends so persuasive and attractive to seekers was they had a message and a way of life—and they lived it. It was not easy or comfortable, but it brought deep community and joy.

A Call and Challenge for Friends Today

What are we learning from the Inward Teacher today? What is faithful action in these challenging, disruptive, discouraging times? I am suggesting that Friends recapture our vision. Picking up on early Friends, who picked up on what Jesus taught, we are not asked to invent or promote a new political or economic system. Instead, we are offered the much more radical and difficult invitation to live into a new social system that is based on *agape* love and compassion.

Keep on doing all the things that tug at your heart, whether it is confronting the construction of a pipeline, cooking meals for the hungry and underhoused, protesting US complicity in the Yemen disaster, uncovering and dismantling white supremacy, supporting legislation to overrule the current termination of environmental protections, sewing face masks to help prevent the spread of the coronavirus, or visiting prisoners. All of this—and so much more—Spirit-led work is vitally important. What is different? We are asked to do everything, every encounter with another human being, each opportunity to interact with another, in a way that is suffused with compassion.

Once, while George Fox was riding through Wales, a "great man" caught up to him and planned to turn Fox in to the authorities as a highwayman at the next town. But Fox was led to speak to him in such a way that the man was moved and instead invited Fox to his house for dinner. Fox explained that the Christ in Fox spoke to the Christ in his opposer.[43] We would probably say that-of-God in me speaks to that-of-God in my neighbor who supports policies that seem to me to be detrimental to human relationships, to economic and social justice, and to the Earth itself. How does that work? It is easier for me to describe it than to actually do it! The idea is to approach with an open heart—not necessarily an open mind—that acknowledges the humanity of the other person. We ask questions rather than make speeches. We are aware that the other may have had experiences that explain her or his opinions. We do not try to make debating points but rather try to make friends. We are not asked to agree with the other's opinions or ideologies but to accept the other person as a bearer of that-of-God within. After all, if there is that-of-God in this other person, how can she not be precious to the Divine, as greatly and unconditionally loved as we are? Have we been granted the authority to disagree with God's choice of whom God loves?

Perhaps the two most difficult places to practice this are in our families and in our meetings. Why is that? Perhaps it is because we are with them so much and they see us in our full range of moods and actions. Perhaps it is because we know they love us, and therefore we can lash out at them without repercussions (or so we hope). Perhaps it is because we unconsciously expect more of our family and meeting than we do of other people. Perhaps we expect them to be like us, or what we would like to be, and when they are not, we get angry. For whatever reasons, families and meetings suffer breaches and quarrels, fights and feuds. Friends can calmly tell Israelis and Palestinians to get along with each other and play nicely but refuse to speak to a sibling or avoid a member of the meeting.

What can we do with our big clay feet, our sharp elbows that poke unintentionally, and our outsized egos that demand recognition? Some sort of transformation seems called for.

Transformation

We need to want to change. If necessary, we can pray for the *willingness* to be changed. What is called for is our transformation, as Paul wrote to the Romans: *Don't be conformed to the patterns of this world: but be transformed by the renewing of your minds so that you can figure out what God's will is—what is good and pleasing and mature* (Romans 12:2 CEB).

Perhaps Paul was pleading. Perhaps he was demanding. Perhaps he was saying you have to choose; either conform to the world as it is or be transformed, but you can't have it both ways. No serving both God and mammon.

On the other hand, a Friend who studies the Bible told me that the Greek for "be transformed" in the New Testament is in the passive voice—as is "be conformed"—and that they both have a sense of ongoingness about them. Interestingly, the Greek verb *metamorphousthe* (met-a-mor-FOOS-the), I'm told, only occurs four times in the New Testament and always in the passive voice: twice it is translated into English as to "be transfigured" (in Mark 9:2 KJV, NRSV, and NIV and Matthew 17:2 KJV, NRSV, and NIV), and Paul's two usages of the word that are translated as to "be transformed" (in 2 Corinthians 3:18 CEB, NRSV, NIV and in Romans 12:2 CEB, KJV, NRSV, and NIV). It seems that both being conformed and being transformed have the sense of a continuing process rather than an instantaneous "conformity" or "transformation." There is almost a sense of un-

26

consciousness about them, not something we *will* to do but something that happens to us.[44]

Sandra Cronk, who I have found to be one of the most important Quaker prophets of the late twentieth century, wrote:

> A transformed life means living in new relationships with others. Indeed, God's healing power often comes to us through the love of others. In this way the church-community is the body of Christ in the world continuing His work of redemption. Thus, a loving community is both an aid in our religious journey and an incarnation of the goal of that journey, i.e. God's Kingdom on earth.[45]

"A transformed life means living in new relationships with others." And here I thought it was just about a cozy relationship between me and God. Fox saw a "great people to be gathered," not just individual souls to be saved. The ongoing work of transformation requires both individual work and the corporate work of a committed community. The goal is not personal salvation to keep me safe in a dangerous world but learning how to live in a way that helps bring the "Kingdom of God" to fulfillment.[46]

Sometimes the invitation to transformation just happens as unexpected, pure grace. One is suddenly held in an embrace of pure, unconditional Love that knows all of our self, accepts us, loves us just as we are, and yet paradoxically invites us to be better. For others—most of us, I suspect—it is a much slower process that draws us, bit by bit, with forgetting and backsliding, toward Something Better, toward Love. Today, if we are willing to resist the blandishments offered in the marketplace of alternatives to help us become "adjusted" to this sick society that Fox called "the world," then the Love/Light/ God/Inner Christ/Spirit—whatever word is used to describe the overwhelming Love we've experienced or yearn for—invites us to become more like itself, more like Love.

Often, this opens a painful process in which the Light shows us those parts of ourselves out of alignment with it. These are the parts we don't want to admit, the ones that, if unexamined, we may project onto others. Margaret Fell famously enjoined Friends:

> Let the eternal Light search you, and try you, for the good of your souls; for this will deal plainly with you; it will rip you up, lay you open, and make all manifest which lodgeth in you; . . . Therefore all come to this, and be searched, judged, led and guided.[47]

The process isn't easy, but it is bound up with Love. Sometimes the Love comes at the beginning as an invitation, sometimes partway along as encouragement, and sometimes not until a lot of internal pain has been felt. Sometimes the Love is a direct mystical experience. Sometimes it comes refracted through other human beings or through nature or music or any experience that touches and opens our soul. I have come to suspect that what touches and opens any one of us is miraculously tailored to what we each are able to perceive and accept.

In my case, it came when I had trapped myself in a pattern of behavior that was detrimental to myself, my family, and my community. I knew it was not good, but I seemed powerless to snap out of it. Then, one day a neighbor courageously confronted me, and I acknowledged to her that she was right. I fled to the basement where I could be alone, and I wept. I'd been primed by an old friend who one wakeful night had told Jesus that she gave up, that she turned her family over to him. In the next days and weeks, a series of remarkable "coincidences" enabled her to learn the magnitude of what she had done and to begin to live into its promise. With her experience in my mind, and feeling faintly foolish but desperate, I got down on my knees and offered myself to

Jesus Christ. Eventually, I emerged from the basement into the backyard and was struck by the beauty of sun and sky and green leaves. George Fox's words came to mind: "and all creation gave another smell unto me than before."[48] I wish I could say I was a new person after that, but there was lots of backsliding, lots of falling down and trying to pick myself up, lots of straying and forgetting to turn back.

What are the difficulties along the way as we move toward a different way of living? John Woolman identified selfishness and greed as the main barriers between us and Divine Wisdom/Love. We might add ego and fear. Woolman named the "natural mind" as human inclination when it is not paying attention to Love. He wrote:

> The natural mind is active about the things of this life, and in this natural activity business is proposed and a will in us to go forward in it. And as long as this natural will remains unsubjected, so long there remains an obstruction against the clearness of divine light operating in us; but when we love God with all our heart and with all our strength, then in this love we love our neighbours as ourselves, and a tenderness of heart is felt toward all people, even such who as to outward circumstances may be to us as the Jews were to the Samaritans.[49]

We are to keep our "natural mind" of greed and selfishness subjected to a focus on loving God, which then enables us to love our neighbors and all people. But this is still a bit opaque for those who have not yet engaged deeply in the process.

Thomas Kelly suggests that the reason for our reluctance, our failure to center down, is not a lack of time in our very crowded days but the "lack of joyful, enthusiastic delight" in the Light that draws us God-ward "at every hour of the day and night."[50] In our haste to love our neighbor, we forget about loving God with all our heart and mind and strength.[51] It is not easy to love Creative Energy, or the Inward Light, or an amorphous "spirit." It may be even more difficult to love the Void, the Great Silence, the Holy Mystery, or the Cloud of Unknowing. Whatever our concept of the Divine is, transformation involves accepting its love and surrendering into it. Accepting its love may be the most important part. Knowing that somehow, some way, you are totally known (even the parts you hide from yourself) and totally loved may be the most important part of the process.

Alcoholics Anonymous as a model

It has been suggested to me that the Holy Spirit's efforts to bring Truth to each generation manifested in the mid-twentieth century with Alcoholics Anonymous (AA). The program distills age-old Truth into language that is accessible in our time. Essentially, it maps out the steps to transformation.

The starting point is admitting we are powerless and our lives have become unmanageable. Why is it that most of us have to be desperate and helpless before we are willing to ask for help? George Fox found that "when all my hopes in them and in all men were gone, so that I had nothing outwardly to help me," he received a response.[52] AA finds a glimmer of hope, as follows: "We came to believe that a Power greater than ourselves could restore us to sanity." There is Something—God—or, as Fox discovered, "a voice that said there is one even Christ Jesus who can speak to thy condition." There is a Power greater than ourselves, regardless of what words any of us choose to describe this Reality. "Sanity" may not be the word I'd choose to describe the state in which I long to be, but it'll do for now.

Next comes the critical step: "We made a decision to turn our will and our lives over to the care of God as we understood him[/her/Light/Spirit]." We face a choice. Yes, I will turn my life over, or no, thanks just the same, I can continue to deal with my life; I'm not *that* desperate. . . yet. A crucial part for today's Friends, who are spread across a wide theological spectrum, is that we do not need to define or even name the One to whom we surrender. As John Heagle points out, "Correct doctrine in itself will not transform attitudes or behavior."[53]

If we say yes, then comes the ripping open Margaret Fell wrote about, or, in AA's language, the step when "we made a searching and fearless moral inventory of ourselves." This can be quite painful. Next is an interesting step for Friends who have done away with ritual confessions. Have we perhaps thrown out the baby with the bathwater? AA continues, "We admitted to God, to ourselves, and to another human being the exact nature of our wrongs." That's not the end, though; we are not to remain stuck wallowing in that muck. "We reach the place where we are "entirely ready to have God remove all these defects of character," and so we go ahead and humbly "ask God to "remove our shortcomings." Note that there are separate steps for coming into the willingness to be changed or transformed and for asking or praying for it to happen. We can't do it by ourselves. We need Divine assistance, and we need to be willing to have this big change.

This isn't the entire program. There are five more steps, and they are all important. If you are not familiar with all twelve steps, I urge you to look them up. The good news is that you don't have to have an addiction to alcohol or some other debilitating dependency—or be in a relationship with someone who is—to use this process. But, you do have to acknowledge your brokenness, which may (or may not) be different from your life becoming "unmanageable." An insatiable yearning for the Inward Light might also be a starting place.

Thomas Kelly sketches four steps into obedience to the Inward Light. First comes "a flaming vision of the wonder of such a life," either through a grace-given personal experience or through meditating upon the lives and words of others to whom such visions have been given. The second step into holy obedience is to begin immediately, right where you are. Right now, sit here in "utter submission and openness" to the Light. Deep inside, "keep up a silent prayer" even while participating in the rest of your life. Third, if you slip and forget—or, rather, *when* you forget, because we all do—just begin again without "anguished regrets and self-accusations." The fourth consideration in holy obedience is to be hands off; no gritting of the teeth and insisting "I will!" "Learn to live in the passive voice . . . and let life be willed through you."[54]

A critical part of AA is that you do not get transformed on your own. You need the help of a Higher Power, and you need other humans. You need some people who are further ahead in the process than you, and you need to reach back and offer a hand to those who are just beginning. It can't be done without a community. If this sounds a bit like developing a system of patrons and clients, the crucial difference is the deliberate lack of dominating power. It is community rather than patronage/clientage. We're all just bozos on the bus, needing and helping one another.

Community

The same dynamic is true for Friends. Perhaps you've heard it said that a single Quaker is an oxymoron—yet how many folks out there claim to be just that? Some resent the possibility that they may be held accountable for their actions or lack of actions. Others find themselves in a meeting that doesn't understand the importance of, and its role in, accountability. Still others live at a distance from Friends and don't feel the urge to try to find kindred souls to begin a new meeting.

Let me reiterate that a transformed *community* is what Paul was talking about; the verb in the phrase *be ye transformed* (KJV) is second person plural. George Fox had a vision of a "great people" to be gathered. We know that a transformed community is made up of transformed individuals. Some work on the personal part first so that they can help the group. Others will come along later, as they see and feel the joy and love of the group. We all need to be working on both parts of it. What really draws us in, draws us toward the Divine like a heliotropic flower turning toward the sun, is Love—Love of both the human *agape* kind and the Cosmic Love that can't really be confined to human words and constructs. That Cosmic Love is like the rain that falls in a parched land on the just and on the unjust.

Morton Kelsey, an Episcopal priest, Jungian therapist, and author, writes that "we can make many true statements about the nature of love culled from the history of spirituality. We can give clear examples of love in action, and we can state how different it is from its imitations." But, the "only way to understand the incredible reality of divine love is to listen to those who have had direct encounters with divine love."[55] This should be a hallmark of all of our meetings—our meeting should be the place we go and the people we want to have conversations with as we share our deepest yearnings for and experiences of Divine Love.

Perhaps a story is the best way to describe Love or Compassion. Connie Green was a hospice nurse. When she was put on the substitute shift, other nurses gratefully passed on to her their most difficult patients. Thus,

A Call to Friends

Connie was assigned to call on Bill, a bitter old grouch nobody liked to visit. Connie did her usual "gut check" before knocking on his door, consciously naming her own issues that might interfere and leaving them outside the room.

> He was grouchy and miserable. I thought to myself, who wouldn't be, alone and dying with all those sick old people! I met him, did the obligatory checking of vital signs and other physical symptoms and sat down for what I was expecting to be a short terse visit. I reflected to this man that it must be really hard to be here, alone and waiting. I put my hand gently over his gnarled old one. After a pause he looked at me and asked if I believed in God. I said yes and he asked me why. I was going to launch into the story of my spiritual encounter when I felt a stop. I was moved instead to simply ask him if he had ever felt unconditional love. He took a deep breath, his eyes filled with tears and he responded very quietly "Right now." We were in the Presence.
>
> It is clear that this is not something I do, rather it may be done through me if I am prepared and willing. Oddly, on reflection, the power of this love is frightening even though in the moment of its flowing it feels as natural as breathing. I think the fear has to do with surrender, knowing that this is not my power and can overcome me at any time. And yet daily I pray "Not my will but Thine be done."[56]

In the words of Paul Christiansen,

> We Friends know the Truth: that we are beloved and that when we give love in return, we lose nothing but gain more. We Friends know the connection that can be built between all people, for we come as ourselves and remain ourselves, but in meeting for worship we are joined in something greater than ourselves.[57]

A Call and Challenge for Friends Today

Love is most obvious for Friends—however rare—in a gathered meeting for worship or business. Steven Davison's 2017 Pendle Hill pamphlet *The Gathered Meeting* is an excellent guidebook on what this kind of meeting is and how to foster it. He writes, "Perhaps the most important factor in fostering a gathered meeting is love."[58]

Learning to live a more God-centered, Christ-filled, Light-infused life is not about rules or guilt or quid pro quo ("*If* I do this, *then* God will do that"). It is about "*because* I have been touched by the Light (or I am one in whom Christ dwells), *therefore* I will do that." The new ways of behavior include compassion, kindness, humility, gentleness, and patience. Joy happens, too. Of course, we are still human, still flawed, and if our meetings are to be beloved communities we must learn to accept others as they are, not as we want them to be—to accept the opportunity to bear one another's burdens. If someone has a short fuse, do we help her bear that burden? If someone is super-sensitive to slights, do we help him bear it? We are reminded that forgiveness is not about justice; it is about healing. Strife too often is the result of disconnecting from Jesus/Love/the Kingdom so that our opinion must be defended, and the divisive issue supersedes our focus on God/Love.[59] Disagreements and conflict are inevitable in any dynamic group; they are not a sign of failure. The important thing is how the community deals with discord.

Qualities of compassion are patience and wisdom, kindness and perseverance, and warmth and resolve.[60] When we turn over our lives to the Spirit, to Love, we discover—somewhat to our surprise—that the fruit of the Spirit is ours. We discover that with increasing frequency we are given—we exude—*love, joy, peace, patience, kindness, generosity, faithfulness, gentleness, and self-control* (Galatians 5:22 NRSV). Faithful living involves bearing one another's burdens and "helping one another up with a tender hand," in the words of Isaac Penington.[61] Abraham Lincoln's words become our mantra: "with malice toward none; with charity for all."[62]

The critical importance of our meetings

Over the decades of my life, as I have examined the "times"—the social, political, and economic systems that govern much of our outward life—I have grieved. And, it has come to me over and over that Friends have the answer to what this hurting world needs so desperately. Or rather, I believe that our fundamental tradition is the antidote to today's ills. This is nothing less than a radical invitation to live in the Kingdom of Heaven of which Jesus of Nazareth spoke. Right here and now, breaking into the corrupt, confused, frightened, sick United States Empire, we are invited to live in a new paradigm. The invitation is plural, to us. We are invited to make our meetings outposts of the Kingdom. Play with the words, use whatever terms you like: kindom, realm, New Order. The critical thing is that together we have put ourselves under the leadership of the Holy Spirit. In Paul's words, *If we live by the Spirit, let us also be guided by the Spirit* (Galatians 5:25 NRSV). Play with the words here, too: Cosmic Love, God, Ground of Our Being, Logos, Inward Christ, Loving Energy, Light—find and use the term that speaks to your condition. The critical thing, though, is *Thy* will, not mine. We come together to demonstrate what a loving community under the direct guidance of Love actually looks like.

This is not a solo enterprise. Nobody can model a new social system alone. We need a group, a meeting, to create a faith community that actually works—and works hard—to love one another, to help one another up with a tender hand, to go forth demonstrating in our homes, schools, workplaces, and spare-time pursuits that there is this whole other way of relating to one another. We are the ones who will discover—together—that there is that within each human that connects with Cosmic Love, that offers instruction and guidance each step of the way into a more loving, compassionate, satisfactory way of relating to other people and to the creation itself. We can do this. It is so simple that healthy small children are doing it automatically. It is also the most difficult thing we will probably ever attempt, and its cost is all. We will be joyful—and always in trouble with authorities who try to uphold the systems, principalities, and powers.

Lloyd Lee Wilson explains,

> God has been calling people, and is still calling us, to be gathered in order to teach us how to be the Kingdom of God, and how to be the seeds for the establishment of the Kingdom of God everywhere. What we do, as we worship and live and do our business together, is we learn those skills and abilities jointly that enable us to model the Kingdom of God to the rest of the world. This is our testimony as a gathered people. And we do God's desire by taking the seeds of that learning out beyond the confines of our monthly meetings and beginning to transform the world outside the Religious Society of Friends.[63]

It is not easy; it takes work. As Sandra Cronk reminds us,

> People will fall. People hurt and wound one another. They turn away from God. The heart of faithful living is to learn how to love on the other side of hurt and betrayal. This is the way of God's forgiving love which restores relationships after there is a break or fall.[64]

If the Society of Friends has anything to offer the world, it is simply the knowledge, the experience, that life is meant to be lived from the Center. This Divine

Center enables each of us to live lives, in Thomas Kelly's words, of "amazing power and peace and serenity, of integration and confidence," provided we really want to.[65] This was the radical transformation undergone by early Friends. Their experiences are well documented through the many journals and writings left by the men and women who went through the tumultuous process. Kelly summarized it (I've edited his gendered language):

> George Fox and the Quakers found a Principle within people, a Shekinah of the soul, a Light Within that lights everyone coming into the world. Dedicating themselves utterly and completely to attendance upon this Inward Living Christ, they were quickened into a new and bold tenderness toward the blindness of the leaders of Christian living. Aflame with the Light of the inner sanctuary, they went out into the world, into its turmoil and fitfulness, and called people to listen above all to that of God speaking within them, to order all life by the Light of the Sanctuary. 'Dear Friends,' writes Fox to his groups, 'keep close to that which is pure within you, which leads you up to God.'[66]

This is our call and our challenge, individually and together: to listen to that Inner Light, to keep close to what it shows us, and to come into obedience to its guidance—as a gathered body.

Endnotes

[1] W. H. J. Gairdner, as quoted in Rufus Jones, *Spiritual Reformers in the 16th and 17th Centuries* (Eugene, OR: Wipf and Stock, 2005), xxvii.

[2] In retrospect, this probably was untrue because she grew up in an intentional community and her parents and the parents of her friends were actively creating an interracial, interdenominational cooperative community in the 1940s and were involved with the American Friends Service Committee and Friends Committee on National Legislation. However, she did not find meetings for worship "on fire."

[3] Revelation 6:1–8.

[4] Genesis 1:28 NRSV, KJV.

[5] John Heagle, *Justice Rising: The Emerging Biblical Vision* (Maryknoll, NY: Orbis Books, 2010), 14.

[6] See, for example, Albert Nolan, *Jesus before Christianity* (Maryknoll, NY: Orbis Books, 1976), 6–8.

[7] Walter Brueggemann, *The Prophetic Imagination* (Minneapolis: Fortress Press, 1978), 21–22, 46–49, 59–61; Timothy Beal, "Why there is no healing without grief," Nov. 14, 2016, The Conversation, http://theconversation.com/why-there-is-no-healing-without-grief-68644; Francis Weller, *The Wild Edge of Sorrow* (Berkeley, CA: North Atlantic Books, 2015), xx–xxi.

[8] Lloyd Lee Wilson said he first encountered the term "implicated resistance" about a decade ago in Serene Jones's 2005 book *Constructive Theology: A Contemporary Approach to Classical Themes*. Email to author, May 27, 2017. It seems to have been coined by Sallie McFague.

[9] Beal, "Why there is no healing without grief." See also Brueggemann, *The Prophetic Imagination*, 59–61; Joanna Macy and Chris Johnstone, *Active Hope: How to Face the Mess We're In without Going Crazy* (Novato, CA: New World Library, 2012), 57–81.

[10] Robert McAfee Brown, *Saying Yes and Saying No: On Rendering to God and Caesar* (Philadelphia: Westminster Press, 1986), 40–42.

[11] Heagle, *Justice Rising*, 18.

[12] For example, see Vicki Constantine Croke, *Elephant Company* (New York: Random House, 2014); Frans de Waal, *Peacemaking among Primates* (Cambridge, MA: Harvard University Press, 1989); Peter Wohlleben, *The Hidden Life of Trees* (Vancouver: Greystone

Books, 2015); Sy Montgomery, *The Soul of an Octopus* (New York: Atria Books, 2015). There are many other examples.

13 For a very insightful and helpful article on anger in today's politicized and polarized United States, see Charles Duhigg, "Why Are We So Angry?" *The Atlantic* 323, no. 1 (Jan./Feb. 2019): 62–75.

14 *The Journal of George Fox*, ed. John L. Nickalls (Cambridge: Cambridge University Press, 1952), 104.

15 Epigraph in Weller, *The Wild Edge of Sorrow*, vi. See also Avichai Scher, "'Climate Grief': the growing emotional toll of climate change," Dec. 24, 2018, NBC News, https://www.nbcnews.com/health/mental-health/climate-grief-growing-emotional-toll-climate-change-n946751, accessed Jan. 21, 2020; Kirsten Weir, "Climate change is threatening mental health," *Monitor of Psychology* 47, no. 7 (July/August 2016): 28, www.apa.org/monitor/2016/07-08/climate-change, accessed Jan. 21, 2020.

16 Weller, *Wild Edge of Sorrow*, 46.

17 Weller, *Wild Edge of Sorrow*, especially pp. 75–88 on rituals in general and pp. 46–53 on a ritual for the sorrows of the world.

18 Lewis Benson, *Catholic Quakerism: A Vision for All Men* (Philadelphia: Book & Publications Committee, Philadelphia Yearly Meeting of the Religious Society of Friends, 1973), 10, 12, 27–30.

19 See John 1:1.

20 John Howard Yoder, *The Politics of Jesus* (Grand Rapids, MI: William B. Eerdmans, 1972), 34.

21 See James C. Scott, *Against the Grain: A Deep History of the Earliest States* (New Haven, CT: Yale University Press, 2017).

22 For this, I draw largely on John Dominic Crossan, *Jesus: A Revolutionary Biography* (San Francisco: HarperSanFrancisco, 1994). For a study of honor in a different context, see Bertram Wyatt-Brown, *Southern Honor: Ethics and Behavior in the Old South* (Oxford: Oxford University Press, 1982).

23 Crossan, *Jesus: A Revolutionary Biography*, 196.

24 Rubem Alves, *Tomorrow's Child: Imagination, Creativity, and the Rebirth of Culture* (Eugene, OR: Wipf and Stock, 2011), 194.

25 Gayle D. Erwin, *The Jesus Style* (Central City, CA: Yahshua Publishing, 1983), 37.

26 Yoder, *Politics of Jesus*, 34.

27 Yoder, *Politics of Jesus*, 38, 69–72.

28 Yoder, *Politics of Jesus*, 66–69, based on work by André Trocmé.

29 Luke 16:1–9; Yoder, *Politics of Jesus*, 73.

30 I'm told that early Mormons established the United Order in which they held all things in common and the bishop's storehouse distributed what was needed.

31 Mabel Dearmer, who opposed Britain's entry into the First World War, died of typhoid helping nurse the wounded of both sides in Serbia in 1915. Mabel Dearmer, *A Deed that Woke the World and Other Stories* (London: Friends' Book Centre, n.d.), 27.

32 This is not to say that all Puritans, Independents, and Round-heads were enamored of the concept of monarchy. See, for example, the radical Putney debates. But they at least understood what Kingdom meant as a metaphor for living under the power and guidance of God.

33 *Journal of George Fox*, 11.

34 *Journal of George Fox*, 104.

35 *Journal of George Fox*, 263.

36 Norman J. Whitney, *Into Great Waters*, William Penn Lecture (Philadelphia: Young Friends Movement of the Philadelphia Yearly Meeting, 1957), 27, 35, 34.

37 See, for example, the testimony of the Lancashire butcher Luke Cock (1657–1740) in *Christian Faith and Practice in the Experience of the Society of Friends* (London: London Yearly Meeting of the Religious Society of Friends, 1960), #42.

38 First World Conference of the Society of Friends, as quoted in Elfrida Vipont Foulds, *Living in the Kingdom*, William Penn Lecture (Philadelphia: Young Friends Movement of the Philadelphia Yearly Meeting, 1955), 3.

39 Third World Conference of the Society of Friends, as quoted in Foulds, *Living in the Kingdom*, 3.

40 Dahr Jamail and Barbara Cecil, "Rethink Activism in the Face of Catastrophic Biological Collapse," *Truthout*, March 4, 2019, https://truthout.org/articles/climate-collapse-is-on-the-horizon-we-must-act-anyway/.

41 Foulds, *Living in the Kingdom*, 18.

42 Kelly, *A Testament of Devotion* (New York: Harper & Brothers, 1941), 31–32. I changed one word to make the quotation more gender inclusive.

43 *Journal of George Fox*, 301–2.

44 Susan Jeffers, email to author, June 13, 2017.

45 Sandra Cronk, "Why I Am Interested in Teaching at Pendle Hill," as quoted in *A Lasting Gift: The Journal and Selected Writings of Sandra L. Cronk* (Philadelphia: Quaker Press of Friends General Conference with The School of the Spirit, 2009), xxv.

46 Lloyd Lee Wilson, *Radical Hospitality*, Pendle Hill Pamphlet #427 (Wallingford, PA: Pendle Hill Publications, 2014), 5–7.

47 Margaret Fell, "An Epistle to Convinced Friends, in 1656," *The life of Margaret Fox, wife of George Fox; compiled from her own narrative and other sources; with a selection from her epistles, etc* (Philadelphia: Book Association of Friends, 1885), 91–92, Digital

41

Quaker Collection, Earlham School of Religion,
http://dqc.esr.earlham.edu:8080/xmlmm/docButton?XMLMMWh
at=builtPage&XMLMMWhere=E10526102.P00000002-
UN&XMLMMBeanName=toc1&XMLMMNextPage=/builtPageFro
mAuthorBrowse.jsp, accessed Feb. 5, 2020.

48 *Journal of George Fox*, 27.

49 John Woolman, as quoted in Michael L. Birkel, *Silence and Witness: The Quaker Tradition* (Maryknoll, NY: Orbis Books, 2004), 28.

50 Kelly, *Testament of Devotion*, 121.

51 Kelly, *Testament of Devotion*, 121–22.

52 *Journal of George Fox*, 11.

53 Heagle, *Justice Rising*, 38–39.

54 Kelly, *Testament of Devotion*, 59–61.

55 Morton Kelsey, *Set Your Hearts on the Greatest Gift: Living the Art of Christian Love* (New York: New City Press, 1996), 44, 45.

56 Connie McPeak Green, unpublished manuscript, 2014.

57 Paul Christiansen, *What We Stand On*, Pendle Hill Pamphlet #429 (Wallingford, PA: Pendle Hill Publications, 2014), 23.

58 Steven Davison, *The Gathered Meeting*, Pendle Hill Pamphlet #444 (Wallingford, PA: Pendle Hill Publications, 2017), 26.

59 James Bryan Smith, *Hidden in Christ: Living as God's Beloved* (Downers Grove, IL: IVP Books, 2013).

60 "Compassion," *Wikipedia*, en.wikipedia.org/wiki/Compassion, accessed March 14, 2019.

61 Isaac Penington [1667], as quoted in *Christian Faith and Practice in the Experience of the Society of Friends* (London: London Yearly Meeting of the Religious Society of Friends, 1972), #404.

62 Abraham Lincoln, "Second Inaugural Address," 1865, Our Documents, https://www.ourdocuments.gov/doc.php?flash=false&doc=38&page=transcript.

63 Lloyd Lee Wilson, *The Exercise of Spiritual Authority within the Meeting* (Lancaster, PA: The School of the Spirit Ministry, 2014), 7–8.

64 Sandra L. Cronk, *Gospel Order: A Quaker Understanding of Faithful Church Community*, Pendle Hill Pamphlet #297 (Wallingford, PA: Pendle Hill Publications, 1991), 26–27.

65 Kelly, *Testament of Devotion*, 116.

66 Kelly, *Testament of Devotion*, 33–34.

Also available from Inner Light Books

Surrendering into Silence: Quaker Prayer Cycles
By David Johnson
   ISBN 978–1-7346300–0-8 (hardcover)
   ISBN 978–1-7346300–1-5 (paperback)
   ISBN 978–1-7346300–2-2 (eBook)

A Guide to Faithfulness Groups
By Marcelle Martin
   ISBN 978-1-7328239-4-5 (hardcover)
   ISBN 978-1-7328239-5-2 (paperback)
   ISBN 978-1-7328239-6-9 (eBook)

A Word from the Lost
By David Lewis
   ISBN 978-1-7328239-7-6 (hardcover)
   ISBN 978-1-7328239-8-3 (paperback)
   ISBN 978-1-7328239-9-0 (eBook)

William Penn's 'Holy Experiment'
by James Proud
   ISBN 978-0-9998332-9-2 (hardcover)
   ISBN 978-1-7328239-3-8 (paperback)

In the Stillness: Poems, prayers, reflections
by Elizabeth Mills
   ISBN 978-1-7328239-0-7 (hardcover)
   ISBN 978-1-7328239-1-4 (paperback)
   ISBN 978-1-7328239-2-1 (eBook)

Walk Humbly, Serve Boldly: Modern Quakers as Everyday Prophets
by Margery Post Abbott
   ISBN 978-0-9998332-6-1 (hardcover)
   ISBN 978-0-9998332-7-8 (paperback)
   ISBN 978-0-9998332-8-5 (eBook)

Primitive Quakerism Revived
by Paul Buckley
   ISBN 978-0-9998332-2-3 (hardcover)
   ISBN 978-0-9998332-3-0 (paperback)
   ISBN 978-0-9998332-5-4 (eBook)

Primitive Christianity Revived
by William Penn
Translated into Modern English by Paul Buckley
   ISBN 978-0-9998332-0-9 (hardcover)
   ISBN 978-0-9998332-1-6 (paperback)
   ISBN 978-0-9998332-4-7 (eBook)

Jesus, Christ and Servant of God
Meditations on the Gospel According to John
by David Johnson

      ISBN 978–0–9970604–6–1 (hardcover)
      ISBN 978–0–9970604–7–8 (paperback)
      ISBN 978–0–9970604–8–5 (eBook)

The Anti-War
by Douglas Gwyn

      ISBN 978-0-9970604-3-0 (hardcover)
      ISBN 978-0-9970604-4-7 (paperback)
      ISBN 978-0-9970604-5-4 (eBook)

Our Life Is Love, the Quaker Spiritual Journey
by Marcelle Martin

      ISBN 978-0-9970604-0-9 (hardcover)
      ISBN 978-0-9970604-1-6 (paperback)
      ISBN 978-0-9970604-2-3 (eBook)

A Quaker Prayer Life
by David Johnson

      ISBN 978-0-9834980-5-6 (hardcover)
      ISBN 978-0-9834980-6-3 (paperback)
      ISBN 978-0-9834980-7-0 (eBook))

The Essential Elias Hicks
by Paul Buckley

      ISBN 978-0-9834980-8-7 (hardcover)
      ISBN 978-0-9834980-9-4 (paperback)
      ISBN 978-0-9970604-9-2 (eBook)

The Journal of Elias Hicks
edited by Paul Buckley

      ISBN 978-0-9797110-4-6 (hardcover)
      ISBN 978-0-9797110-5-3 (paperback)

Dear Friend: The Letters and Essays of Elias Hicks
edited by Paul Buckley

      ISBN 978-0-9834980-0-1 (hardcover)
      ISBN 978-0-9834980-1-8 (paperback)

The Early Quakers and 'the Kingdom of God'
by Gerard Guiton

      ISBN 978-0-9834980-2-5 (hardcover)
      ISBN 978-0-9834980-3-2 (paperback)
      ISBN 978-0-9834980-4-9 (eBook)

John Woolman and the Affairs of Truth
edited by James Proud

      ISBN 978-0-9797110-6-0 (hardcover)
      ISBN 978-0-9797110-7-7 (paperback)

Cousin Ann's Stories for Children by Ann Preston
edited by Richard Beards
illustrated by Stevie French

ISBN 978-0-9797110-8-4 (hardcover),
ISBN 978-0-9797110-9-1 (paperback)

Counsel to the Christian-Traveller: also Meditations and Experiences
by William Shewen

ISBN 978-0-9797110-0-8 (hardcover)
ISBN 978-0-9797110-1-5 (paperback)